MESSIAH'S STAR

Morning stars together proclaim your holy birth...

By

Michael Leonard Dourson

June 17, 2014

Copyright Notice

Published by Michael Leonard Dourson
http://messiahsstar.com

Cover by Elizabeth Mackey and Dan Dourson

TABLE OF CONTENTS

PREFACE

For the harvests of the Spirit, thanks be to God. For the good we all inherit, thanks be to God. For the wonders that astound us, for the truths that still confound us, most of all, that love has found us, thanks be to God.[1]

This story is about the star of Bethlehem. Parts of this story are based on Biblical narratives, including text from the Old Testament, the Gospels of Matthew and Luke, and the Book of Revelation. Other parts of the story are based on astronomical events now known to have occurred around the time of the birth of Jesus of Nazareth, using the research of many investigators and the free astronomical software Stellarium©[2]. Still other parts are based on the political and cultural contexts of Jewish and other ancient peoples. And finally, parts of this story are based on the biology of human conception, for after all, this is the story of a human birth.

This story includes hypothetical conversations among various Biblical characters, including Zachariah and Elizabeth, the magi (wise men or "kings"), Mary and Joseph, and Herod and his court. These conversations have been developed to mesh, but honor, the Biblical, astronomical, political, cultural, and biological contexts. Our tale begins with an angel's visit to a Jewish man during the spring of the year 3 BC[3], includes a birth that happens during the summer of 2 BC, and ends with the safe arrival of the Holy Family in Nazareth after the death of King Herod in the winter of 1 BC.[4] This story offers one interpretation of what the magi saw in the night skies that caused them to journey to Jerusalem. It also shows when Jesus may have been born and why the famous star appeared to stop for a time over the little town of Bethlehem. It is hoped that these insights will allow the reader to gain a meaningful and powerful understanding of the conjunction of nature and Biblical text documenting this blessed birth.

The story may not include all pertinent facts, and several of its interpretations may be improved or changed with further thought and discussion. As with any attempt at understanding the Messiah's star, several assumptions are made. First, it is assumed that the natural law (nature) and the written law (the Bible) have the same dignity and teach the same things in a way that one of them has nothing more, nothing less, than the other (St. Augustine, 354–430). It follows from such an assumption that both the Bible and nature need to be studied to gain insights into the star of Bethlehem. In our study of nature, the conjunctions that occurred near the birth of Jesus and our understanding of the biology of human conception and birth should both be viewed in light of their relevance to the Biblical text. It is also assumed that the inspired word of the Bible, in its various translations, reflects what actually occurred but was written using the terminology that was most appropriate at that time. The dialogue in this text gives particular attention to several of the more critical Greek words that formed the original language of the scriptural text.

Did the wise men really follow a star that led them to the baby, Jesus? If so, what did the star look like? How was it different from other stars? The people of that time used the stars and the astronomical occurrences to guide their lives in a powerful way. What were the anomalies in the normal astronomical observations that would cause the magi to travel to the court of King Herod and boldly ask where the new Jewish king was?

The answers to these questions have been explored from a study of the Bible and related texts, have been ignored altogether, or have just been accepted as Biblical truth without further thought. The star of Bethlehem has also been analyzed as a conflation of pagan and Christian ideas in an attempt to justify belief in Jesus. In contrast to these approaches, let the words of St. Augustine motivate us all to pause and consider both the Bible and nature, and in particular the biological and astronomical evidence, in our quest for understanding.

About stars, constellations, planets, conjunctions and backward motion

Most of us give little thought to how the heavens work, other than the sun rising in the east, setting in the west and changing position in the sky according to the seasons. Our knowledge of the movements of the moon is usually limited to its waxing and waning. Few know what a blue moon or a blood moon represents. Many people likely could not point out more than five constellations in the heavens on any given night.

However, this has not always been the case. People of Jesus' time knew the movements of the planets and the constellations very well and taught them to their children. Many of them slept on their rooftops or outside during the summer nights. And since no outdoor lighting existed, the night sky was seldom obscured by light pollution. Modern society would be considered as ignorant as young children in the time of Jesus if this lack of understanding of the heavenly bodies was openly expressed.

At night the heavens contain a vast array of stars visible to the naked eye. They appear to us in constellations to which we give fanciful names. These stars are actually moving, but they are so very far from

Earth that they do not appear to be doing so. For the purposes of this story, we will consider them fixed and not moving. Two of them play a prominent role in our story: the sun and Regulus, a prominent star in the constellation Leo. You will learn more about Regulus later in the story.

The heavens also show to the naked eye on any given night Earth's moon and/or five planets: Mercury, Venus, Mars, Jupiter and Saturn. The moon and all five planets play a role in the story of the Messiah's star. The planets, sometimes called wandering stars, move around the sun in the same direction and on the same plane as Earth, much like bits of cocoa float around the top of hot chocolate as it is stirred. Because some planets are farther from the sun, they appear to move more slowly though the sky, for example, Saturn is the farthest and appears to move the slowest. In addition, because Earth is moving around the sun at a rate that is different from that of the other planets, the planets sometimes appear to move backwards against the field of fixed stars as Earth moves past them, much as a car appears to move backward when you pass it on the highway. This happens once a year with each of the planets beyond Earth and more than once a year with planets closer to the sun than Earth is. Of course, because this apparent backward motion happens after an obvious forward motion, at some point the planet appears to stop. Jupiter did just this at a very interesting time during our story. Sometimes these planets appear to be close to each other or, more rarely, to touch each other. When this happens, the closeness is termed a conjunction.

Why are we only now hearing this evidence?

The simple answer is that we now have software that allows us to look back in time at the motion of these five planets, the moon and the sun. We can literally and without question know the positions of these seven lights in the sky at any point in history and from any place on Earth. This is possible because the mathematics of planetary motion are known (and have been known for several centuries) and the software, which has been generally available in only the last couple of decades, easily does all the complex calculations that allow positioning of these seven lights in the sky on our computer screens. The United States National Aeronautics and Space Administration (NASA) uses this same mathematics to plan planetary travel even today.

When we use this software to observe the skies around the time of Jesus' birth, the heavens open up and, visually, declare the glory of God. In fact, the years 3 BC and 2 BC were rich in the number of close conjunctions visible from Earth, the frequency of which is perhaps unmatched at any other time.[5] The list of conjunctions during these two years is shown in Appendix Table 1. Interestingly, the Bible text had a few "conjunctions" of its own during this time that precisely overlap with the scientifically documented conjunctions and biology of human conception, as described in the story.

But first, the author is indebted to the scholarship of several previous investigators, specifically Ernest Martin, author of The Star That Astonished the World (1998), Frederick Larson, creator of the Web site and video at http://www.bethlehemstar.net, Susan S. Carroll, author of The Star of Bethlehem: An Astronomical and Historical Perspective (undated) and Dwight Hutchinson, author of the well-researched and recent book, The Lion Led the Way (2013). In particular, conversations with Chris Dourson, Dwight Hutchinson and Allen Johnson have been very helpful in understanding the underlying Jewish customs and holidays, and in verifying several of the astronomical conjunctions and Hebrew and Greek words. The Biblical events described in this text are found mostly in the Revised Standard Version of the Bible (Oxford University Press, 1962). The astronomical events described all happened on the date given, as found in Martin (1998, page 66) with several minor corrections made from Stellarium©. Gregorian calendar dates that match important Jewish dates can be found at http://www.fourmilab.ch/documents/calendar with adjustments given by Hutchinson (2013).

And finally, I have been ably assisted by my brother, Dan Dourson, and Elizabeth Mackey, who provided the artwork for the book cover; Judy Dourson and Ellen Dawson-Witt who gave many necessary edits; and my much better half, Martha Dourson, who listened to countless rehearsals and made many suggestions for improvement, as God's spirit moved me to finish this work.

Footnotes

1. Third verse of the song "For the Fruit of All Creation" by Fred Pratt Green. b. 1903.

2. Stellarium 0.12.4, copyright 2000–2013, Stellarium Developers.

3. BC is the acronym that means "Before Christ", and is used exclusively throughout this story. However, many scholars acknowledge that Jesus was likely born before the year 1. Scholars also refer to these BC years as BCE, or before conventional era.

4. Ernest Martin (1988) promotes the idea that King Herod died in 1 BC, rather than 4 BC, which had been the prevailing view. A 1 BC death of King Herod allows us to consider the conjunctions between the years of 4 BC and 1 BC in our quest for understanding the events leading to the birth of Jesus.

5. Perhaps once in 4 to 5 billion years; an approximation of this occurrence is a straightforward calculation based on the individual occurrences of events. See Appendix Table 3 for information that allows the estimation of the likelihood of all related events occurring in one and a half years of 3 BC to 1 BC.

CHAPTER 1

The First Announcement

The heavens are telling the glory of God; and the firmament proclaims his handiwork. Day to day pours forth speech, and night to night declares knowledge. There is no speech, nor are there words; their voice is not heard; yet their voice goes out through all the earth, and their words to the end of the world. (Psalm 19: 1-4)[6]

The Jewish year 3758 (3 BC) in a city of Judah

Winter had finally yielded to spring now that the start of the Jewish year, Nisan 1 (March 17), was well past. An elderly priest named Zachariah gathered his belongings in preparation for a second trip to Jerusalem for his temple duties. His first trip at Passover was uneventful. He would be gone this time for the better part of two weeks because his Abijam division of the priestly line not only had duty the eighth week of the Jewish year, but also would be working the following Festival of Weeks. He kissed his wife, Elizabeth, goodbye and reminisced about their lovemaking just before his first trip. Even if we are advanced in years, he thought, we get this occasional joy. And as so often done before, but now mainly out of habit, he sent a silent prayer heavenward about their special request for a child.

He traveled to Jerusalem and started duty on the Sabbath, Saturday 26 of Iyyar, the second Jewish month (May 9). Zachariah's first week of work was as uneventful as Passover had been. His second week of duty was quite the opposite, however. Because this was a high holiday of the Jewish nation, the Festival of Weeks, which Christians would later call Pentecost, "the whole multitude of the people" [Luke 1:10] was clearly in evidence and priestly duties seemed to be never ending.

And then, the unexpected happened.

Zachariah learned on Tuesday (May 19) that he had been chosen by lot to enter the Holy Place of the Jewish Temple on the morning of the next day and offer incense on behalf of the Jewish nation [Luke 1:9]. Quite literally, Zachariah would be the voice of the Jewish people before the Lord, offering incense and prayers for the whole nation. For a short time, he, Zachariah, would be considered by some to be the Jewish protector.

What an honor---and responsibility! Such an assignment generally occurred only once during a priest's lifetime of service, and not every priest was so blessed. Many of his colleagues had waited in vain for this honor. Zachariah would have to wait as well, but only to tell Elizabeth. He was heady with the honor bestowed on him, and it consumed nearly his whole thinking the rest of the day.[7]

He awoke well before dawn on the following morning and learned from the temple magi of an unusual, and brief, observation of a conjunction that very morning of the planet Saturn, known as "Rest," or "Sabbatical," by Jews and as "the Jewish Protectorate" by Gentiles, and the planet Mercury, known as "the Sun's Scribe" by Jews and as "God's Messenger" by Gentiles. Saturn's Jewish nickname (among many others) was perhaps because it was the slowest of the seven visible moving lights in the sky---and because of our penchant for resting on the Sabbath, Zachariah thought. Mercury's Gentile nickname (among many others) was because it was closest to the sun and was the quickest moving of the visible planets. He wondered, but only fleetingly, of what significance this possible conjunction could be. His duty beckoned!

As Zachariah entered the Holy Place to offer incense before the Temple sacrifices on the morning of May 20, he was filled with trepidation. Would he perform his duties correctly? Had not Aaron's sons and several others been struck dead when they hadn't done the job as instructed? [Leviticus 10:1–2] As his eyes adjusted to the three main religious objects inside, the altar on which incense was burned, the table with bread offerings, and the candlestick with seven branches, he was startled to see someone standing at the right hand of the altar. Did he somehow come in during the wrong time? However, taking in the visage standing before him, his surprise changed to sheer terror.

And then the angel spoke.

> Do not be afraid, Zachariah, for your prayer is heard, and your wife, Elizabeth, will bear you a son, and you shall call him John. And you will have joy and gladness, and many will rejoice at his birth; for he will be great before the Lord, and he shall drink no wine nor strong drink, and he will be filled with the Holy Spirit, even from his mother's womb. And he will turn many of the sons of Israel to the Lord their God, and he will go before him in the spirit and power of Elijah, to turn the hearts of the fathers to the children, and the disobedient to the wisdom of the just, to make ready for the Lord a people prepared. [Luke 1:13–17]

Recovering himself somewhat, Zachariah said to the angel, "How shall I know this? For I am an old man, and my wife is advanced in years." [Luke 1:18]

And the angel answered him, "I am Gabriel, who stands in the presence of God and I was sent to speak to you and to bring you this good news. And behold, you will be silent and unable to speak until the day that these things come to pass because you did not believe my words, which will be fulfilled in their time." [Luke 1:19–20]

And so the first recorded miracle of the Christian New Testament came to pass. Zachariah was struck dumb.

The angel left.

It was only after this ordeal and the mix of excitement, terror and joy had slowly subsided that Zachariah realized he could not speak. And then it slowly dawned on him the significance of the conjunction between Mercury and Saturn. God's Messenger had indeed visited the Jewish Protectorate![8]

When Zachariah's time of service ended, he returned home to share the joyous news with Elizabeth. As he entered his house, she came to him glowing and radiant. He was overjoyed to see her but also surprised. There was something about her that was different, and then he noticed her enlarged breasts. Perhaps she is just excited to see me, he briefly thought.

Elizabeth could hardly contain herself as she relayed her symptoms to him. In her distress, she barely noticed that he had not uttered a word to her. She was always too hot, her breasts were sore and swollen, she was frequently nauseated and she seemed fatigued. As Zachariah listened, he became more excited. Were these not the symptoms of a pregnant woman? Gabriel was right: Elizabeth was pregnant. His joy knew no bounds as he tried to relate Gabriel's visit and news, but then stumbled in his efforts. Elizabeth abruptly stopped talking and realized that Zachariah could not speak. She retrieved a writing tablet, and Zachariah's effort to tell his story took an immense amount of time.

Finally understanding, Elizabeth exclaimed, "Zachariah, it is just as the angel said, our prayer has been heard for now I know I am pregnant and my joy, like yours, has no bounds. But I fear the scorn of men, who will look at me and say that I only give the appearance of being pregnant so that my reproach will be taken away. I wish to hide myself until the birth."

Arguing with Elizabeth proved futile, especially when one could not speak. And so it came to pass that "Elizabeth [knew she was pregnant][9] and for five months she hid herself." [Luke 1:24]

The third Jewish month, Sivan, 8 (May 20, 3 BC) in Babylon about 700 miles away

A young apprentice ran excitedly down the stairs into the room below the terrace of the ziggurat in the Marduk Temple of Babylonian[10] where the senior magi were having a brief breakfast of sweet, juicy dates and fresh water. "Master Gaspar, we are having an unexpectedly visible conjunction of Saturn and Mercury in the constellation Taurus. Please come see before the morning sunrise."

His morning breakfast interrupted, Gaspar went upstairs with his excited apprentice and looked eastward. His eyes were not as sharp as they were once, but looking at early morning conjunctions always warmed his heart. The Sun's Scribe, or the Messenger, Mercury, was indeed in conjunction with Saturn, Rest, or the Jewish Protectorate, and the constellation Taurus was clearly waning as the morning sky brightened.

"What does it mean?" the young apprentice asked.

"That's a good question." And continuing in the magus tradition, Gaspar stated, "What do you think? What do our records show?"

The apprentice responded. "Such a conjunction in the morning between Saturn and Mercury occurs only about once in 30 years, but I do not know the significance of it occurring in the constellation Taurus. Do you, Master Gaspar?"

And Gaspar answered, "Hmm… Perhaps a messenger from God sent to a Jewish person of some importance. But what the message is, I do not know."

His apprentice replied, "Oh, if only the stars would speak to us of these things, so that we might not have to guess."

Gaspar smiled, "But, of course, they do, young man; they just do not use words."

Footnotes

6. Just how might the heavens declare the glory of God, utter speech and reveal knowledge, without speech or their voices being heard? At first reading this passage seems incomprehensible, and various translations have changed this text to get around this seeming impasse. But what if the text is meant to be read in this way? After all, this is the Bible. In fact, do we not, each one of us, often reveal knowledge, without speech or our voices being heard? Of course, we do. You are now

---

reading symbols on a piece of paper (or electronic format) to receive information. Is it, perhaps, in the use of symbols that the heavens declare the glory of God? That is an interesting idea, but if correct, one needs to figure out what the symbols might be. Perhaps before we explore the star of Bethlehem, we need to investigate possible symbols associated with it, and specifically with the planets Mercury, Venus, Mars, Jupiter and Saturn, the sun and Regulus, and the constellations Virgo and Leo. These "symbols" also have common nicknames that appear to be highly relevant to the Star of Bethlehem story, as shown in Appendix Table 2.

7. Zachariah's priestly division of the Abijam (i.e., the eight division, Luke 1:5) conducted Jewish temple duties twice a year starting at Nisan 1, the beginning of the Jewish new year. Each priestly division also worked all three major festival weeks (Passover, the Festival of Weeks, and the Day of Atonement). In 3 BC Nisan 1 fell on what would be our March 17 (see Appendix Table 4). Priests started duty the Sabbath (Saturday), so the first division started its work on March 14, and the 8 division would have started its work on May 9, nine weeks later, which is the 8 week of priestly duty, since all priests worked the week of Passover (and thus this week is not counted). The Abijam division would also be working the week after May 16 because this was the Festival of Weeks (the holiday that Christians now refer to as Pentecost) when all priests also worked. That this feast was likely occurring is consistent with the phrase "and the whole multitude of the people" [Luke 1:10], which may indicate a larger than the expected crowd at temple duty than during non-holiday weeks.

8. Is this a coincidence? Or did the heavens declare the glory of God in sending Gabriel to Zachariah at the time of this poignant conjunction?

9. In this passage, the Greek word for "conceive" incorporates the concept of "capture" and has been

---

interpreted as "being certain that she was to become a mother" (Basic English Bible). The accuracy of this interpretation is derived from the fact that Elizabeth hid herself for five months immediately afterwards, which would have been unlikely immediately after presumed conception---because pregnancy often takes some time to be noticed by a woman, especially if she is "well along in years" or menopausal. But hiding herself for five months fits with the description of Elizabeth being four months pregnant at the arrival home of Zachariah in late May or early June, and with Elizabeth being six months pregnant in the sixth month of the Jewish year, Elul (or our August). This interpretation would place the birth of John the Baptist during the month of November, 3 BC, five months after Zachariah returns home to Elizabeth from his priestly duty. The conclusion from this biological and scriptural analysis is that Elizabeth was pregnant at the time of Gabriel's visit with Zachariah and that she realized that she was pregnant after Zachariah's return from duty, and not that she conceived at this time.

10. The author is indebted to the work of Hutchinson (2013, page 247) for this insight on Babylonian temples.

CHAPTER 2

A Betrothal

The fourth Jewish month, Tammuz, (June 13, 3 BC) in Nazareth

A warm June evening was upon the festive gathering as the two families got to know each other better. The pledging of marriage was always a blessed occasion, but this one seemed more so because, quite by happenstance, another conjunction had occurred in the morning skies on this very day, this time between Saturn and Venus, known as "Brightness" by Jews and as "the Mother" by Gentiles (among many other names).

A friend remarked, "Joseph, you are a lucky man. Mary is a lovely young lady. And how did you manage to arrange your pledge of marriage on a day of this wonderful conjunction?"

"Just part of God's design, no doubt," Joseph replied. But then he privately thought, This is really very interesting. Just last month Mary said that her kinsman, a priest name Zachariah, had a vision of an angel during his temple duties on the very day of a conjunction of Saturn and Mercury. Now we have a conjunction of Saturn and Venus. I wonder what this means.[11]

What a handsome man, Mary's mother thought. So kind and considerate.

Mary's father's thoughts were more pragmatic: Joseph has a fine reputation as a carpenter and people admire his work. He will be able to provide well for Mary and their children. The fact that he is somewhat advanced in years will only add to his ability to take care of them.

In Babylon

The young apprentice, Simon, ran excitedly down the stairs into the room below the terrace of the ziggurat. "Master Gasper, as you predicted, Saturn is now in conjunction with Venus in the constellation Taurus. Please, come see."

The early morning meal complete, Gaspar went upstairs with his excitable apprentice and again looked eastward. Saturn was indeed now in conjunction with Venus in the constellation Taurus as the morning sky brightened. Saturn had been approaching Venus for over a week, but the chance of this conjunction was not known with certainty until this morning.

"What does it mean, Master Gaspar?" the young apprentice asked.

"That's a good question. What do you and your young colleagues think?" replied Gaspar.

Simon responded. "A conjunction of Saturn and Venus occurs more frequently than that of Saturn and Mercury, which we saw last month, about once in seven years in the morning, but I do not know the significance of it occurring in the constellation Taurus. However, may I hazard a guess, Master?"

"Why, of course, please explain yourself," replied Gaspar.

"Well, I think it has something to do with the birth of the Jewish Messiah. To begin with, we have the prophecy of our great ancestor, Daniel, in which he wrote, and I am quoting, sir, from the Book of Daniel:

> Seventy weeks of years are decreed concerning your people and your holy city, to finish the transgression, to put an end to sin, and to atone for iniquity, to bring in everlasting righteousness, to seal both vision and prophet and to anoint a most holy place. Know therefore and understand that from the going forth of the word to restore and build Jerusalem to the coming of an anointed one, a prince, there shall be seven weeks. Then for sixty-two weeks it shall be built again with square and moat, but in a troubled time. And after

> the sixty-two weeks, an anointed one shall be cut off, and shall have nothing, and the people of the prince who is to come shall destroy the city and the sanctuary. (Daniel 9:24–26)"

Simon continued, "If this is to be interpreted as 70 weeks of years between the building of our glorious city Jerusalem and the death of the anointed one, as directed for us to consider in Leviticus 25:8, then this would be 490 years. We know that the Temple was rebuilt in the year of Ezra's commission in 3303 (458 BC), so it follows that the anointed one would be cut off, or killed, in the year 3793 (33 AD)."[12]

Gaspar replied, "So what does this have to do with our conjunctions, Simon?"

"Well," said Simon, "If the anointed one is killed in the year 3793, he must have been born prior to this, and these conjunctions might indicate this."

And Gaspar thought, My young apprentice is turning into a fine young magus. And then answered, "Simon, this is an interesting speculation, but it is now the year 3758 (3 BC), so can the anointed one be so very young when he is to be killed, or perhaps he has already been born? Does our scripture state his age when he is to be cut off?" Gaspar knew that it did not, but couldn't resist this additional testing.

"No" said Simon. "It does not, at least from my readings."

"Well then, perhaps we need some additional signs from the heavens, if we are to interpret them as a sign of the anointed one's birth. These two conjunctions are very interesting, Simon, and not very common, as you have correctly stated, especially when seen only one month apart. Please let me know if you think of anything else."

And then Gaspar walked down the stairs of the ziggurat of the temple and on to his morning's work.

Footnotes

11. One might speculate that this conjunction represented the betrothal of Joseph, here representing the Jewish Protectorate (or Saturn) and Mary as the future mother (or Venus) based on Luke 1:27 and the use of the past tense of the verb betroth. This date of Joseph and Mary's betrothal, however, is not found in other existing Biblical text.

12. The author is indebted to the work of John Pratt for this synthesis (Meridian Magazine, 15 September, 2004).

CHAPTER 3

A Star Seen in the East (At Its Arising)

The sixth Jewish month, Elul, 3 (August 12, 3 BC) in Babylon

The commotion in the ziggurat where the early morning astronomical observations were made was unmistakable through Gaspar's bedroom window across the courtyard. All week long, morning observations indicated the approach of Jupiter, known to Jews as "Righteousness," or "Justice," and to Gentles as "The King" (among many other names) and Venus. And several had speculated about a possible conjunction. Simon, and his colleagues were giddy with excitement, and even now Gaspar heard one of them running up the stairs to his room. He feigned sleep.

The apprentice outside his door hesitated. He was shortly joined by a colleague who said, "Simon, you must awaken Master Gaspar."

Simon shuddered, knocked on the door, and entered. "Master Gaspar, it is Simon. I know that it is early and that you are not feeling well, but you need to see something." Gaspar had no need to make the young man feel bad, so he roused himself and said, "Thank you, Simon, I was already awake, and I look forward to your findings."

Simon left the room and Gaspar put on his long, comforting robe. The apprentices were barely able to contain themselves but kept mum. As he entered the courtyard, he saw the shadows first---where no shadows should have been seen before sunrise. As he rounded the building, he saw it. A lustrous, brilliant, pulsing, gorgeous Venus, the same morning star as in the June conjunction, had swung toward the sun but had now caught up with a nearly equally lustrous, brilliant Jupiter. He had seen one previous morning conjunction of these morning stars together, but never this close, in fact, so close that he could see only one bright, extended light. But he knew that the younger men should be able to tell them apart, barely, and their conversations confirmed it.[13]

Gaspar's first thought after the shock of this unexpectedly close conjunction faded was, My goodness, this is the third conjunction in nearly as many months. Can this be the star of the anointed one? I must send a message to Melchior and Balthasar.

"Simon, come quickly," Gaspar exclaimed. "Please eat breakfast, and then take this message to Masters Melchior and Balthasar. 'Have we seen the star of the anointed one at its arising? Do these morning stars together, proclaim his holy birth?'"[14]

.....

The argument among the senior magi lasted 20 days. Gaspar was convinced that this conjunction of Jupiter and Venus was the star of the anointed one. It came on the heels of two prior conjunctions, one involving Saturn and Mercury, and one involving Saturn and Venus. Scripture confirmed that a virgin mother would bear the anointed one. And these three conjunctions, within four months, appeared to be signifying this. Moreover, the timing of these conjunctions was consistent with the prophesy of Daniel, as Simon, his apprentice, had already suggested. Melchior was partial to Gaspar's argument, but Balthasar was unmoved. The conjunction was not clearly in the correct sign.

Why in Cancer," he asked? "Cancer signifies the end of the age. Would not the Messiah's sign be found well inside of Leo, the beginning? Besides, if the timing of your young apprentice, Simon, is correct, Gaspar, then the Messiah would be killed at a very young age, only 34 years. This is hardly time to overthrow the Roman government that is besetting the Jewish nation and to shepherd in a new age."

"True enough," Gaspar rejoined, "but the conjunction is at the boundary of these two constellations of Leo and Cancer, as you well know, Balthasar, and so can be seen as the beginning of a new age."[15] So he was not swayed by Balthasar's argument.

But in the end, it was the stars that resolved the impasse. As the argument had proceeded, the morning observations revealed yet another pending conjunction, this one between Mercury and Venus. On the morning of August 31, these two planets were found in close conjunction in the constellation Leo, the constellation associated with the tribe of David of the Jewish nation.

"What does it mean, Master Gaspar?" Simon asked.

"We seem to be trying to answer this question a lot, Simon," Gaspar mused. "What do you think?"

Simon responded, "Such a conjunction in the morning occurs only about once in six years. But now we have had four visible conjunctions of the planets, which fit within our ancestor Daniel's prediction, in four months. The occurrence of these four conjunctions so close together is only about once in every 15,000 years.

"Indeed, this grouping of conjunctions is very rare," Gasper answered, "But what do you think this latest conjunction means, Simon?"

Simon answered, "A messenger from God sent to a woman of the Jewish tribe of David, perhaps, especially since the conjunction is in the sign of Leo. But what the message is, I do not know."

Yes, but I do know, thought Gasper. It is time to tell our emperor, Phraates IV.[16] Melchior and Balthasar will come around. We need to prepare for a trip to Jerusalem.

Footnotes

13. This date is very likely to be the first observation of the "star" (the Jupiter-Venus conjunction), as described in Matthew 2:2: "Where is he born king of the Jews? For we have seen his star in the East, and have come to worship him." Also "in the east" is the Greek *te anatole,* literally meaning "the rising," which would be consistent with the first observation of the conjunction in the early morning because this is when such astronomical events are first observed. Four other Biblical references seem to confirm this event:

Numbers 24:17. "I see him, but not now; I behold him, but not nigh: a star shall come forth out of Jacob, and a scepter shall rise out of Israel"

Isaiah 60:3. "And nations shall come to your light, and kings to the brightness of your rising." Here the Greek words for "light," "brightness" and "rising" can be interpreted as "star," "Venus" and "dawning" respectively. Other interpretations are possible.

Peter 1:19. "You will do well to pay attention to this as to a lamp shining in a dark place, until the day dawns and the morning star rises in your hearts."

Revelation 22:16. "I, Jesus, have sent my angel to you with this testimony for the churches. I am the root and the offspring of David, the bright morning star."

14. O Little Town of Bethlehem, verse 2, Phillip Brooks (1835–1893).

15. I am indebted to Dwight Hutchinson (2013, page 135) for this insight.

16. Ibid, page 78.

CHAPTER 4

The Second Announcement

The sixth Jewish month, Elul, 22 (August 31, 3 BC) in Nazareth

It was morning, and Mary was happy. To be betrothed to Joseph was such a blessing. Her wedding would be within the year. She sang softly to herself as she prepared for morning prayers.[17] Stepping from her bedroom, she was startled to see what appeared to be a man.

> And he came to her and said, 'Hail, O favored one, the Lord is with you!"' But she was greatly troubled at the saying and considered in her mind what sort of greeting this might be. And the angel said to her, "Do not be afraid, Mary, for you have found favor with God. And behold, you will

> conceive in your womb and bear a son, and you shall call his name Jesus. He will be great, and will be called the Son of the Most High; and the Lord God will give to him the throne of his father David, and he will reign over the house of Jacob for ever; and of his kingdom there will be no end."
>
> And Mary said to the angel, "How shall this be, since I have no husband?"
>
> And the angel said to her, "The Holy Spirit will come upon you, and the power of the Most High will overshadow[18] you; therefore, the child to be born will be called holy, the Son of God. And behold, your kinswoman Elizabeth in her old age has also conceived a son; and this is the sixth month with her who was called barren. For with God nothing will be impossible."
>
> And Mary said, "Behold, I am the handmaid of the Lord; let it be to me according to your word."
>
> And the angel departed from her. [Luke 1:28–38]

Mary could not think clearly. And the more she replayed her encounter with what, an angel, in her head, the more she worried. Whom could she tell? Her father? Her mother? Would they understand? She realized that they might, especially in light of Uncle Zachariah's encounter with the angel Gabriel earlier in the year. But what about her friends, the village, and oh . . . Joseph? How could she explain all of this when everyone would consider the obvious reason for her pregnancy to be fornication---a grievous sin, a sin punishable by stoning? Could she live with this shame? Would she even live?

In turmoil she again recalled the angel's words, and then an answer came to her. Yes, her aunt Elizabeth was six months pregnant! Why had her mother not told her? Was this the angel's confirmation of his words to her? Elizabeth would understand. And as all of these thoughts jumbled together, Mary steeled herself to speak with her parents. She needed to see Elizabeth and to somehow talk with her Uncle Zachariah. She wanted him to describe the appearance of his messenger.

Footnotes

17. The morning of August 31, 3 BC, Mercury (God's Messenger) was in conjunction with Venus (Mother). The Bible shows this "conjunction" as Gabriel (God's messenger) visiting Mary the future mother (Luke 1:26-37). "In the sixth month the angel Gabriel was sent from God to a city in Galilee named Nazareth." (Luke 1:26) Note that the sixth month referred to here is often thought to be referring to Gabriel's statement in verse Luke1:36 that Elizabeth is in the sixth month of her pregnancy with John, the future Baptist. At first reading, however, this seems to be an odd connection. Why not the sixth month of the year? In fact, a more likely interpretation is that Luke is relaying Mary's description of the angel's visit to her as during the sixth month of the Jewish year, Elul, which would not be unexpected because Mary was a Jewish maiden. This passage would likely also be understood as the sixth

---

month of the year when first read because the reference to six months of Elizabeth's pregnancy is only after this text. It might also be read as the sixth month of the Jewish year, if Theophilos, the stated audience for the gospel of Luke, were a Jewish Sadducee (see for example, http://en.wikipedia.org/wiki/Theophilus_biblical). Finally, astronomically, it is in the month of Elul, the sixth month, in which the conjunction of Mercury and Venus falls. This interpretation of the sixth month being Elul can also be seen in:

Hastings, James (Editor). 2004. *A Dictionary of Christ and the Gospels. Volume I, Part One.* Aaron to Excuse. ISBN: 1-4102-1785-X. University Press of the Pacific. Honolulu, Hawai'i. Page 410.

Benson, Rev. C., 1819. *Birth, Baptism, and Crucifixion of Jesus Christ.* Trinity College. Cambridge University Press. Page 97. Based on the work of Allix de Christi anno et mense natali. 8vo. 1707.

18. Here the Greek word for overshadow is *episkiazo*, which means "to cast a shadow upon" or "to envelop in a haze of brilliance." This same word is also used to describe the transfiguration of Jesus (Matt 17:1–5), and, thus, its use in Luke 1:35 may more likely refer to the haze of brilliance rather than a shadow. Thus, the angel states that Mary will be enveloped in a haze of brilliance as she conceives, which figuratively and literally happens two weeks later as described in the next chapter.

CHAPTER 5

Conception

Patmos in the Aegean Sea (late first century)

John, the youngest of the twelve apostles of Jesus, was now an old man. The years of his walking with Jesus and being referred to as a "son of thunder" were distant, but fond memories. His exile was difficult but not any more so than that of any of the other apostles, and he alone still lived, very much in keeping with Jesus' response to Peter's question about John on the shore of Lake Galilee so very long ago when Peter asked "Lord, what about this man?" [John 21:21]

John's visions had continued through the night, so after a sparse breakfast, he again started writing. "And a great portent appeared in heaven, a woman clothed with the sun, with the moon under her feet, and on her head a crown of twelve stars; she was with child and she cried out in her pangs of birth, in anguish for delivery." [Revelation 12:1–2] John knew that many of his readers would understand his vision. The constellation Virgo (the virgin) was clothed[19] with the sun (the father) every year around September and the Jewish holiday of Rosh Hashanah, the Feast of the Trumpets. It was likely no different in September of the year that the Virgin Mary conceived Jesus.

The seventh Jewish month, Tishri, 1 (September 11 3 BC) in Nazareth[20]

Mary's parents had believed her story about the angel's appearance in part because Mary could not possibly otherwise have known that Elizabeth was pregnant. Elizabeth told no one but her closest family before she went into hiding, and Mary's mother had not shared this news with anyone but her husband. But Mary's father insisted she would have to wait to visit Elizabeth until after the two-day Rosh Hashanah celebration starting on September 11 (Tishri 1). It was not appropriate for her to miss this important holiday with her now-extended family. Joseph's concerns were important now that they were betrothed. Besides, Mary's father thought to himself, This may have been a vivid dream and she really is not pregnant. But if she is, at some point, Joseph will have to be told.

As Mary was helping to prepare for the evening festivities of Rosh Hashanah, she felt the sudden urge to rest. And after walking into her parents' garden, she lay down on a bench in the late-afternoon September sun and became enveloped in the haze of its brilliance. Awakening a short time after the sun set from a sensual dream, she sensed something was different, and a feeling of intense well-being permeated her spirit. The celebration of Rosh Hashanah was marvelous, but the morning following the second day of celebration brought a bout of nausea. She worked through this as she prepared for her visit to Elizabeth, and after thanking her parents again for their understanding, and recognizing that Yom Kippur, the Jewish Day of Atonement, was only a few days away, Mary . . .

> went with haste into the hill country, to a city of Judah, and she entered the house of Zachariah and greeted Elizabeth. And when Elizabeth heard the greeting of Mary, the babe leaped in [Elizabeth's] womb; and Elizabeth was filled with the Holy Spirit and she exclaimed with a loud cry,
>
> Blessed are you [Mary] among women, and blessed is the fruit of your womb! And why is this granted me, that the mother of my Lord should come to me? For behold, when the voice of your greeting came to my ears, the babe in my womb leaped for joy. [Luke 1: 39–44]

And Mary remained with Elizabeth for about three months until John's birth was to occur.[21] [Luke 2:56] During her visit, she spoke to Zachariah several times, and he in return used his tablet to write down his thoughts. Although communication was difficult, it ended with both of them agreeing that the angel of her visit was likely Gabriel, the same messenger from God who had visited Zachariah. The fact that these visits came on the same days as the conjunction of Saturn and Mercury in the case of Zachariah, and the conjunction of Venus and Mercury in the case of Mary, was only fitting.

Did not the heavens declare the glory of God?

---

19. In the evening of September 11, 3 BC the constellation Virgo was behind the sun from the perspective of Earth. A Biblical reference to this event is described in Revelation 12:1, in which a virgin (in this case Virgo) is being clothed with the sun. What does it mean to be clothed in the sun? Walk outside on a cloudless day during daylight hours and what do you see in the sky besides the sun? Unless the moon is at least partially full, you will see only blue skies and the sun because the sun's light is so overpowering as to "clothe" all other lights in the sky. And, assuredly, many other lights are there, as more than amply demonstrated during a solar eclipse when the sun's light is blocked by the moon. On September 11, 3 BC, Virgo was clothed in the sun, which occurs yearly over a period of several weeks. However, in 3 BC, September 11 also happened to be the Jewish holiday, Rosh Hashanah. The angel Gabriel foretold of this future event after Mary asked how she might conceive without having sexual relations with a man. (Luke 1:35: And the angel said to her, "The Holy Spirit will come upon you, and the power of the Most High will overshadow you."). Thus, Gabriel states that Mary will be enveloped in a haze of brilliance as she conceives, as per the previous footnote, she agrees, and this enveloping in a haze of brilliance happens in the heavens less than two

---

weeks later when the constellation Virgo (the virgin) is clothed by the sun (Father). A new crescent moon just happens to be at her feet between 6:15 pm and 7:45 pm on September 11, just as described in Revelation 12:1. The conclusion from this biological, astronomical, and scriptural analysis is that Mary conceived on September 11 between 6:15 pm and 7:45 pm in the evening. Three other references are consistent with this timing:

Luke 1:38. Here Mary agrees to Gabriel's word indicating that her conception will be at a future time.

Luke 2:21. Here reference is made to the name given by the angel before Jesus was conceived, again indicating that conception would occur after Gabriel's visit with Mary.

Luke 2:7. A birth occurs nine months after September 11th, 3 BC, as described in Chapter 7 of this book.

20. I am indebted to both Ernest Martin (1998) and Dwight Hutchinson (2013) for this date and several others in 2 BC, which does not match with the previously cited calendar converter:

http://www.fourmilab.ch/documents/calendar

21. An unusual statement is made in Luke 1:57–58: "Now the time came for Elizabeth to be delivered, and she gave birth to a son. And her neighbors and kinsfolk heard that the Lord had shown great mercy to her, and they rejoiced with her." The unusual feature of these two verses is the implication that her neighbors and kinsfolk did not know that Elizabeth was pregnant. However, these two versus make sense if Elizabeth hides herself for five months (Luke 1:24) after she realizes that she is four months pregnant when Zachariah returns home from duty.

CHAPTER 6

Pregnancy

The seventh Jewish month, Tishri, (September 14,3 BC) in Babylon

Gaspar's time with Emperor Phraates IV proved to be fruitful, and Melchior and Balthasar were supportive. Gaspar explained to the emperor that they had seen four conjunctions in the prior months. The first conjunction, between Mercury and Saturn, signified a meeting of God's messenger and a Jewish person of some importance. The second conjunction, between Saturn and Venus, indicated a meeting of a Jewish person of some importance and perhaps the virgin from whom the Messiah was prophesized to be born. The third conjunction, between Jupiter and Venus might signify the holy birth or perhaps a sign of the birth to come---Gaspar and Balthasar still disagreed on this point---but both agreed that these morning stars together announced a holy birth. The fourth conjunction between Mercury and Venus indicated a meeting of God's Messenger and the Mother-to-be. This was one argument in favor of Balthasar's view because there might be no need for a fourth conjunction if the prior one indicated that the birth had occurred.

Gaspar summarized his argument to Emperor Phraates IV by saying that while each one of these conjunctions had been seen at a previous time, no magus alive had seen these four conjunctions in as many months. And as Gaspar explained to the emperor, these conjunctions, especially the last two in or near the constellation Leo, indicated that the Jewish nation was involved, and Jewish scripture indicated that a virgin would give birth to the Messiah. Daniel, one of the more significant figures of Babylon's ancient court, prophesied that the Messiah would be born around the present time. However, Gaspar saved the most powerful argument for last.

"Just this morning, Your Excellency, we confirmed a fifth conjunction, this one between Jupiter and Regulus, known to us and magi nearly everywhere as "the King Star." Although this conjunction occurs every dozen years or so, it comes at a time of these four other conjunctions. Moreover, Jupiter, the King, is in conjunction with the King Star in the constellation Leo, which---did I mention this already?---is a sign of the Jewish tribe from whence the Messiah is to come, and is occurring during the Jewish high holy days. This conjunction is a powerfully confirming sign. We need to prepare for a trip to Jerusalem to honor the new Jewish Messiah."

Gaspar had argued well. Emperor Phraates IV agreed and preparations were started for a trip to Jerusalem. Because this was to be an official visit, much preparation was needed. And each night, Jupiter continued its western movement through the field of fixed stars. Western leading, still proceeding,[22] thought Gaspar. And just the direction we will be taking to Jerusalem. How appropriate.

February 17, 2 BC and May 8, 2 BC, evenings in Babylon

Preparations were well underway. The entourage would have as the dignitaries Gaspar, Melchior and Balthasar. They would be accompanied by their apprentices, a contingent of soldiers, and the ever-necessary porters and cooks. The whole trip would take the better part of a year because the wandering route between Jerusalem and Babylon was approximately 1000 miles and horses could travel only about 15 miles per day. Thus, the trip just to Jerusalem would take the better part of two months. And, of course, they would be expected to meet and greet King Herod and his court, and there would be numerous meetings of fellow magi and other officials before their visit to the newborn king. Then, of course, they would greet the newborn king. The return trip would be equally long.

One of the early decisions concerned the gifts one should bring to the Jewish king. Balthasar argued that gold and frankincense were essential because this would fulfill an ancient prophecy:

> And nations shall come to your light, and kings to the brightness of your rising.... They shall bring gold and frankincense, and shall proclaim the praise of the Lord. [Isaiah: 60:3; 60:6]

Melchior and Gaspar concurred. In addition, Melchior argued for myrrh, an expensive and fragrant perfume, because the prophecy of Daniel predicted that the Messiah was to be cut off and have nothing. Thus, the gift of myrrh, often associated with burials, would be appropriate:

> And after the sixty-two weeks, an anointed one shall be cut off, and shall have nothing. . . . (Daniel 9:26)

In early February, Earth's rotation around the Sun caught up to Jupiter's rotation around the sun, and when viewed in the night sky, Jupiter appeared to slow down against the field of fixed stars. Jupiter then stopped, and then appeared to go backwards against the field of fixed stars as Earth passed it. On February 17, 2 BC, this apparent backward motion again brought Jupiter in conjunction with Regulus. Yet another confirming sign, thought Gaspar: a double conjunction of Jupiter and Regulus in the sign of Leo. And then Gaspar realized that after Jupiter's backward motion was complete, it would again stop and start back in a westwardly direction and would likely make another conjunction with Regulus. He was not surprised when Simon announced that a third conjunction of Jupiter and Regulus occurred during the evening observations on May 8.[23]

"Have you ever seen such a triple conjunction of Jupiter and Regulus, Master Gaspar?" ask Simon.

"No," Gaspar answered, "and neither has anyone else of whom I am aware." Their preparations for the trip to Jerusalem were nearly complete.

Footnotes

22. We Three Kings of Orient are, verse 1, Reverend John Henry Hopkins, Jr., (1857).

23. During the nights of September 14, 3 BC, February 17, 2 BC and May 8, 2 BC Jupiter made three separate conjunctions with Regulus. A triple conjunction of Jupiter with a fixed star is not an uncommon occurrence. A triple conjunction of Jupiter with a particular star, however, is rare. This triple conjunction occurred between Jupiter, the King planet, and Regulus, the King star, in the constellation of Leo, the sign of Judah of the tribe of David from whence would come the Messiah of the Jewish nation. After the September 14 conjunction, Jupiter proceeded its westwardly course through the fixed stars and then appeared to stop and go backwards as Earth's rotation overtook Jupiter's. This apparent backward motion caused Jupiter to make a second conjunction with Regulus on February 17, 2 BC. After passing Regulus a second time, Earth completed its passing of Jupiter, and Jupiter went back into normal westwardly motion against the field of fixed stars from Earth's perspective, and made a third conjunction with Regulus on May 8, 2 BC. Note that the planet Jupiter was farther in the west each night in its normal motion against the fixed background of stars,

perhaps leading to the inspiration of a phrase in a popular Christmas song about the visit of the magi (see previous footnote).

CHAPTER 7

The Messiah's Birth

The third Jewish month, Silvan, 15 (June 17, 2 BC) in Bethlehem[24]

"Mary," Joseph said, "the inn has no room, but the inkeeper says that we are able to use the stable, at least until a room becomes available. Will this be alright?"

Joseph had long ago resolved to follow the advice of an angel that appeared to him in a dream to take Mary as his wife. [Matthew 1: 20–21] But his choice had lead to much scorn. That Joseph could not wait until the proper time to consummate his marriage was the common, and polite, wag. Other rumors held that Mary had a dalliance with a younger man when she was visiting Elizabeth. On the few occasions Joseph stated that the child was the product of the Holy Spirit, he was ridiculed. He resigned himself to be held in scorn, but he often questioned how this son, Jesus, was to grow up and lead the Jewish nation when some would refer to him as a bastard. [John 8:41]

The decree from Caesar Augustus that all the world should be enrolled [Luke 2:1] was another in his and Mary's seeming misadventures. Joseph had argued that a pregnant woman should be allowed to forgo the enrollment because traveling from Nazareth to Bethlehem was unwise. But in the end, Joseph lost the argument and the trip began later than required.[25] Now that they had arrived safely in Bethlehem, there was no room at the available inns, even though the celebration of the Week of Festivals was already past. The only consolation of this whole enterprise seemed to be in that the heavens were once again showing a pending conjunction, between Jupiter and Venus. In fact, the common perception among the populous was that the conjunction would be closest tonight. He comforted himself with this thought and unpacked his and Mary's belongings in the stable.

Mary's cry of distress brought a sense of urgency to his activity, and a hasty request to the innkeeper to find a mid-wife.

> And [Mary] gave birth to her first-born son and wrapped him in swaddling cloths, and laid him in a manger, because there was no place for them in the inn. [Luke 2:7]

> And in that region there were shepherds out in the field, keeping watch over their flock by night.[26] [Luke 2:8]

"What a gorgeous night," exclaimed the first shepherd. "I have never seen a more stunning conjunction of these two wandering stars, Jupiter and Venus. What could it signify?" A second shepherd responded, "I do not know, but turn around and look to the east. It is also a full moon on the rise. So now you have two questions to answer." The western conjunction became more visible as the sun set and the full moon rose above the horizon. The usually dark landscape was alit as it had never been seen before, or since, in recorded history.

All is calm, all is bright, thought the first shepherd. This is a night to remember. And then,

> An angel of the Lord appeared to them, and the glory of the Lord shone around them, and the [shepherds] were filled with fear. And the angel said to them, "Be not afraid; for behold, I bring you good news of a great joy which will come to all the peoples; for to you is born this day in the city of David a Savior who is Christ the Lord. And this will be a sign for you: you will find a babe wrapped in swaddling cloths and lying in a manger." And suddenly there was with the angel a multitude of the heavenly host praising God and saying, "Glory to God in the highest, and on

> earth peace among men with whom he is pleased." [Luke 2:9-14]
>
> When the angels went away from them into heaven, the shepherds said to one another, "Let us go over to Bethlehem and see this thing that has happened, which the Lord has made known to us." And they went with haste, and found Mary and Joseph, and the babe lying in a manger. And when the [shepherds] saw it they made known the saying [Glory to God in the highest…] which had been told them concerning this child; and all who heard it wondered at what the shepherds told them. But Mary kept all these things, pondering them in her heart. And the shepherds returned, glorifying and praising God for all they had heard and seen, as it had been told them. [Luke 2:15–21]

In Babylon

Preparations were over. All that was needed was for Gaspar, Melchior and Balthasar to agree on a date to leave. Balthasar insisted that the birth had not yet occurred, and Gaspar and Melchior were inclined to believe him. But as they debated, the answer again came from the stars. All of them were aware that Jupiter was again on its westwardly movement through the field of fixed stars after its third conjunction with Regulus. And now Venus appeared from behind the sun in the evening skies on an approach that that seemed to beckon Jupiter. Could it happen that these two wandering stars would again form a conjunction?

That these planets would form yet another conjunction was highly improbable. No one could remember anyone having seen these two planets form two conjunctions in any one year. But they had already seen seven conjunctions to date all within one year. The odds of these seven conjunctions occurring in one year were, well, astronomical. In fact, Simon had estimated the occurrence of these seven conjunctions close together as once in about 570,000 years.

Balthasar finally made a wager that the first conjunction of Jupiter and Venus had been on the boundary of Cancer, the sign of the end of an age, and Leo, the beginning of a new age. It would be only fitting for Jupiter and Venus to again make a conjunction well within the sign of Leo, the beginning. Neither Gaspar or Melchior took up the wager, however. Collectively they sensed that Balthasar was correct. It was only a matter of waiting for the conjunction to occur. Such a conjunction occurs once every 12 years in the evening, thought Simon, but this conjunction, if it were to occur along with the other prior seven conjunctions, would happen only once in about 7 million years. Could the heavens be this old?

And as Balthasar predicted, the conjunction did occur, on June 17, 2 BC. As Jupiter completed its westwardly journey through the field of fixed stars, it joined with Venus, so close, in fact, that not even the young magi could tell them apart. The western display of this conjunction as the sun set was stunning. No one had ever seen a star so very bright.

But the event was made even more glorious when the full moon rose on the eastern horizon, as the senior magi knew it would. And a prophecy occurred to Gaspar:

> Once I have sworn by My holiness; I will not lie to David. His descendants shall endure forever and his throne as the sun before Me. It shall be established forever like the moon, and the witness in the sky is faithful. [Psalm 89: 35–37][27]

And so the full moon witnessed the conjunction of Jupiter and Venus. Never before (or since) had the glory of the Lord shown so brightly all around humankind. And the magi and their apprentices were humbled and awed.

"He is born," Balthasar said. "We leave tomorrow." [28]

Footnotes

24. Hutchinson (2013) argues that the year 2 BC had the intercalary month of Adar II before Nisan. Thus, I have used his information for Jewish dates in the year 2 BC.

25. Much has been written about this census, which was apparently complete during the spring of 2 BC (see Martin, 1998 and Hutchinson, 2013). The completion of the census in the spring of 2 BC makes a June date for a trip to Bethlehem by Joseph and Mary seem unreasonable. However, censuses were generally conducted locally, so all local governments in all

---

regions probably did not implement this decree simultaneously (Keener, 1993, Bible Background Commentary, New Testament, InterVarsity Press, Downers Grove, IL, page 193).

26. Keeping watch over their flock by night is consistent with shepherds grazing their flocks at night (Keener, 1993, page 194), which may have been more likely because of the heat of the summer days in Bethlehem.

27. I am indebted to Dwight Hutchinson (2013, page 166) for this insight. The quoted Bible is the New American Standard Bible.

28. Jupiter (Righteousness or King) is once again in conjunction with Venus (Brightness or Mother), but this time in the evening. Jesus is born as described in Luke 2:8–9. Three lines of evidence confirm that Jesus was born on this date.

The first line of evidence comes from a synthesis of scripture and astronomy. Note that verse 9 of Luke refers to the glory of the Lord shining around them. This would be expected because the Jupiter-Venus conjunction in the western sky was one of the brightest "stars" seen in human history. The planets were 0.01 arc degree apart, which is too close to be separately distinguished but not so close for Venus to block Jupiter's light. So the western sky was lit up. But this was also the night that a full moon rose in the eastern sky perhaps inspiring a phrase in yet another popular Christmas song about the birth of Jesus (i.e., Silent Night, verse 1, "All is bright").

The second line of evidence comes from a synthesis of astronomy and biology. The fact that the moon was at a crescent on September 11, 3 BC, the date of conception, and was full on June 17, 2 BC, the date of Jesus' birth, is consistent with a fetus coming to full term at birth.

The third line of evidence has three parts all of which come from a synthesis of scripture and biology. Luke 2:1–3 refers to a census necessitating travel, which would most reasonably occur during the warmer months (but see Martin, 1998, and Hutchinson, 2013, who argue for the summer/fall of 3 BC). Luke 2:8 also refers to shepherds tending their flocks at night, which, again, would most reasonably occur during the warmer months. However, the most compelling reason for accepting the third line of evidence, and indeed, the most compelling evidence for this date as Jesus's birth, is the underlying biology of human conception. June 17, 2 BC is exactly 40 weeks, the average time of human pregnancy, from Jesus' conception on September 11, 3 BC…to the *very* day.

CHAPTER 8

Fateful Meetings

The fourth Jewish month, Tammuz 26 (July 28, 2 BC) in Jerusalem

Jesus was circumcised 8 days after his birth according to Jewish custom. Mary and Joseph had to wait an additional 33 days for Mary to complete her ceremonial uncleanliness and then all three of them went to Jerusalem on what would have been July 28 for their purification, according to the law of Moses.

> Now there was a man in Jerusalem, whose name was Simeon, and this man was righteous and devout, looking for the consolation of Israel, and the Holy Spirit was upon him. And it had been revealed to him by the Holy Spirit that he should not see death before he had seen the Lord's Christ. [Luke 2:25–26]

The prior month had seen the spectacular conjunction of Venus and Jupiter, and with a full moon. Tales of a marvelous birth and angels near the town of Bethlehem had been circulating. Simeon thought to himself, If the Messiah had been born on that night, then his parents might be bringing the boy to the Temple for their purification rite on this very day.

> And inspired by the Spirit he came into the temple; and when [Mary and Joseph] brought in the child Jesus, to do for him according to the custom of the law, . . . [Luke 2:27]

Simeon asked them, "When and where has this child been born?"

Joseph answered, "It was on the night of the wonderful conjunction of Venus and Jupiter in Bethlehem."

Simeon tried hard to control his building excitement and then asked, "Are you aware of the stories circulating about a birth in that town associated with the appearance of angels to shepherds tending their flocks at night."

Joseph acknowledged, "Yes, this is the very birth and Jesus is this very child. The shepherds visited us that same night and brought us tales of great joy that included announcements from angels. It was all quite overwhelming." Then,

> [Simeon] took [Jesus] up in his arms and blessed God and said, "Lord, now

> lettest thou thy servant depart in peace, according to thy word; for mine eyes have seen thy salvation which thou hast prepared in the presence of all peoples, a light for revelation to the Gentiles, and for glory to thy people Israel." And [Joseph and Mary] marveled at what was said about [Jesus]; and Simeon blessed them and said to Mary his mother, "Behold, this child is set for the fall and rising of many in Israel, and for a sign that is spoken against (and a sword will pierce through your own soul also), that thoughts out of many hearts may be revealed." And there was a prophetess, Anna, the daughter of Phan'u-el, of the tribe of Asher; she was of a great age, having lived with her husband seven years from her virginity, and as a widow till she was eighty-four. She did not depart from the temple, worshiping with fasting and prayer night and day. And coming up at that very hour she gave thanks to God, and spoke of him to all who were looking for the redemption of Jerusalem. [Luke 2: 28–38]

Out of Babylon to Jerusalem

As expected, the journey to Jerusalem was long, but not overly arduous, especially when traveling at night in the moonlight to avoid the summer heat. The entourage was well protected by the contingent of soldiers, and all of the towns visited along the way were happy to see the magi and their colleagues.

Unfortunately, but as expected, they lost their guiding star, Jupiter, as it set below the horizon on July 28. Yet another confirming sign, thought Gaspar. This day coincides not only with the setting of Jupiter in the western evening skies, but also with the conjunction of the sun and Regulus below the western horizon. Might this coincide with the purification rites of the newborn king and his mother? It is 41 days since the birth of the Messiah, and this is the minimum time needed for the purification ceremony. [29]

And Simon thought, All of us will be joyful as Jupiter reappears in the morning skies in a few weeks.

The magi and their entourage arrived in Jerusalem on August 19, nine weeks after the Jupiter-Venus conjunction that signified the holy birth, and went about finding rooms and meeting with minor dignitaries, a necessary prelude to meeting with King Herod.

Gaspar, Melchior and Balthasar met briefly with King Herod on August 26, 2 BC. They chose this date to meet with King Herod because in the morning skies a conjunction of Mars, Jupiter and Mercury was appearing, with Venus close by, and all agreed that this conjunction, even though it was partially obscured in the morning glare of the sun, was also of significance.[30] Simon, the budding mathematician in the group, noted that the frequency of such an occurrence was about once every 78 years and then calculated that the occurrence of these nine conjunctions together again would not be for another 540,000,000 years.

As they entered the hall of King Herod, they exclaimed how happy they were to be in Jerusalem. After the ceremonial introductions, including a greeting from Emperor Phraates IV to King Herod read by Balthasar, King Herod's magi described the fruits of their preliminary discussions. Finally getting a chance to speak, Gaspar got to the point of their visit.

> Where is he who has been born king of the Jews? For we have seen his star in the east [at its arising], and have come to worship him. [Matthew 2:2]

Although prompted by his senior magus at an earlier private meeting to expect this question, "When Herod the king heard this, he was troubled, and all Jerusalem with him." [Matthew 2:3] Herod thought, Are not these same signs, evident for all to see, being interpreted by everyone in the Roman empire as being associated with the elevation of Caesar Augustus to the Father of all Nations? In fact, have not these magi come during a census for making allegiance to Caesar, the very process of which is now being completed?

Herod thanked the magi for their interest in the newborn Jewish king and promised a full meeting of the Jewish chief priests and scribes to fully answer this important question. However, such a meeting would take some time to arrange, and so he offered the magi the most opulent accommodations available for dignitaries of Emperor Phraates IV.

Herod wasted no time in sending emissaries to all Jewish chief priests and scribes in Judea. He quickly found out, however, that a meeting with these Jewish men and the magi would have to wait until after the upcoming Jewish high holidays, including Rosh Hashanah, Yom Kippur (the Day of Atonement), and Succoth (the Feast of Tabernacles). Although a wait until late October was not at all desirable to the magi, it did allow them to participate in the Jewish holidays in Jerusalem, the home of their ancestors. And, of course, they were obliged to acquiesce to the wishes of King Herod.

Herod also asked his temple guards and spies for information regarding any unusual events surrounding the purification rites of newborn babies in the last several months. This information was not long in coming. The following day, Herod's chief guard stated, "Just during the last month of Tammuz [July], Your Excellency, a man named Simeon and a prophetess named Anna made a commotion in the temple at the purification rites of young boy from Bethlehem born in the preceding month. The boy was from a very poor couple because they offered only two pigeons for the required sacrifice. And as you will recall, we had that spectacular conjunction of Jupiter and Venus that same month. We heard a story about angels appearing to shepherds abiding their sheep by night because of the heat of the day, but who believes shepherds? Besides, both Simeon and Anna are old. So we thought nothing of this commotion and did not think it wise to bother you."

Herod thanked his guard and thought of what he might do to find the child secretly. But then decided that it might be best to allow the magi to visit the child and his parents first and then take action, if needed, after the magi left. After all, there was no overt reason for upsetting dignitaries of Emperor Phraates IV, and the child would not be hard to find.

After the Jewish holidays, Herod invited the magi back to his audience and

> Assembling all the chief priests and scribes of the people, he inquired of them where the Christ was to be born. They told him, "In Bethlehem of Judea; for so it is written by the prophet: And you, O Bethlehem, in the land of Judah, are by no means least among the rulers of Judah; for from you shall come a ruler who will govern my people Israel." [Matthew 2:4-6]

The meeting with King Herod ended, and Gaspar, Melchior and Balthasar went away perplexed. How is it, they exclaimed to each other, that the Jewish magus, chief priests and scribes did not associate these signs with the birth of their Messiah. Rather, Herod's senior magus had tried to convince Gaspar, Melchior and Balthasar that these signs had something to do with the Roman Caesar Augustus. These polite discussions between the three senior magi and their counterpart from Herod's court continued for many weeks after their second meeting with Herod, but always it seemed to Gaspar, Melchior and Balthasar to have a sinister undertone.

Finally, in December

> . . . Herod summoned [Gaspar, Melchior and Balthasar] secretly and ascertained from them what time the star appeared; and he sent them to Bethlehem saying, "Go and search diligently for the child, and when you have found him bring me word, that I too may come and worship him." [Matthew 2:7–9]

But Herod knew all along what he would do if he found the child, which is what his secret meeting with the three magi without his magus, chief priests and scribes was intended to discover. Herod owed his allegiance to Caesar, and it would be maintained at all cost.

This child would have to die.

Footnotes

29. According to Dwight Hutchinson (2013, page 196), such a dual event occurred only infrequently and confirmed the prophesy of Daniel that proclaimed the arrival of the Messiah at the culmination of "62 sevens" of years.

30. August 26, 2 BC, might be the date of the first meeting of the magi with King Herod in Jerusalem. This is possibly represented in the heavens by a conjunction

of Mars (Blushing or god of war), Jupiter (Righteousness or King), and Mercury (Scribe or Messenger), with Venus (Brightness or Mother) nearby.

The first line of evidence for a meeting on this date is from a synthesis of biology and astronomy, but the biological aspects depend on the origin of the magi. For example, if the magi were from the East near Babylon, they and their entourage would have taken at least two months to travel the approximately 1000 miles to Jerusalem (about 15 miles per day on horses). Arriving at Jerusalem would likely have been a big deal, involving lots of dinners, meetings and trading of gossip and other information. This series of meetings and dinners would likely have taken several months especially since the Jewish high holidays were also occurring during this time. The astronomical part of this first line of evidence is that this is a conjunction of four planets, one of them known as the god of war. This conjunction might signify a meeting between Herod and three senior magi.

A second line of evidence for this date is scriptural. Note the odd choice of the word "troubled" in Matthew 2:2. If Herod and "all of Jerusalem" were not aware of the astronomy of the time, then would not the word "surprised" be more appropriate? Moreover, Herod had to have at least one magus in his employment, and it would have been the height of incompetence if this magus missed these rather obvious astronomical signs. In fact, Martin (1998) states that everyone in the Mediterranean basin was hugely aware of the astronomy at that time, and importantly, considered the changes to be associated with the elevation of Augustus, the current emperor in Rome, to "father of all nations." In light of Martin's argument, the census that Luke talks about in Chapter 2 perhaps makes more sense, if the census is seen as making allegiance to Caesar, rather than for a taxation. Thus, the magi's

---

interpretation that the astronomical signs were associated with a Jewish king would be "troubling" to Herod, not being Jewish, and his staff, because it would indicate that their focus on what was important to Rome was misplaced.

CHAPTER 9

To Stop a Star

The ninth Jewish month, Kislev 28 (December 25, 2 BC) in Jerusalem

As expected by all magi, Jupiter had arisen from being clothed by the sun at their first visit to King Herod and his court in August and had again become a morning star.[31] During subsequent weeks, Jupiter started its normal westwardly movement through the field of fixed star as seen in early morning observations, which Gaspar and his contingent had continued to make. When the time came to conclude their conversations with King Herod and his court, and after their secret meeting with King Herod, Earth's rotation around the sun caught up to Jupiter's rotation.

And as Earth caught up to Jupiter, Jupiter appeared to slow down its nightly movement in the field of fixed stars, and then when Earth lined up straight between the Sun and Jupiter, Jupiter stopped.

"Master Gaspar, Jupiter is coming to a stop in the constellation Virgo, southwest of our position in Jerusalem."

"Thank you, Simon," replied Gaspar. "What is the nearest town located in this position?"

"Bethlehem is directly underneath Jupiter," replied Simon, "and Bethlehem is just a short distance southwest of Jerusalem on a main road. It is just as the chief priests and scribes described where the Messiah was to be born."

And Simon thought, Jupiter stopping in Virgo occurs about once every 12 years. Therefore, the likelihood of all of these events ever happening again is about once in 6,500,000,000 years. But Simon then thought, No wait, these events happened over one and one half years, so the likelihood is really once in about 4,300,000,000 years. The heavens are very old, indeed.

And Gaspar thought, Lo, the star which we had seen in the East goes before us, till it comes to rest over the place where the child is.[32] [Matthew 2:9] How appropriate. Gaspar relayed this information to Melchior and Balthasar and "when they saw the star [stopping], they rejoiced exceedingly with great joy." [Matthew 2:10]

Balthasar then recommended to Gaspar and Melchior for a small delay in their visit to Bethlehem so that their arrival coincided with the Jewish holiday, the

Feast of Dedication (or Hanukkah), when gift exchanges were the norm. Gaspar and Melchior agreed.

The subsequent trip to Bethlehem was somber and stately. But it did not take long. When Gaspar, Melchior and Balthasar inquired about an unusual birth in the near past, the townsfolk readily directed them to the house of Joseph and Mary. The shepherds' tale had not been forgotten. Arrangements were made to stay for a few days, and a messenger was sent to Joseph to arrange for a meeting. The excitement of being so close to their goal after more than a year of preparation and journey was palpable amongst the entourage.

The next day, December 25, Jupiter was stopped in the field of fixed stars at the early morning observation. Gaspar, Melchior and Balthasar, with a selected few apprentices and several soldiers, walked down the narrow streets and up to the house of Joseph and Mary.

> And going into the house they saw the child with Mary his mother, and they fell down and worshiped him. Then, opening their treasures, they offered him gifts, gold and frankincense and myrrh. [Matthew 2:11][33]

"What is the child's name?" Gaspar asked.

"His name is Jesus, as indicated by the angel," Joseph spoke.

And Gaspar responded with a quotation from Isaiah,

> I bring near my *deliverance*, it is not far off, and my salvation will not tarry; I will put *salvation* in Zion, for Israel my glory. [Isaiah 46:13]

Then Gaspar explained to Joseph and Mary that this scripture was highly relevant because the word for "deliverance" was the same as for the wandering star Jupiter, which was the main star that showed the magi the way to Bethlehem and the very one that stood above Bethlehem when they looked at the heavens from Jerusalem. Moreover, the word for "salvation" was yeshua, or Jesus, the very name given to the child by the angel. [34]

After the giving of gifts, the magi retired for the day, but not before asking Joseph whether they could further discuss the events leading up to the birth of Jesus. Consent was given, and over the next several days Gaspar, Melchior, Balthasar, Joseph and Mary discussed the signs leading up to the birth. And all during this time, Jupiter remained motionless in the heavens.

The discussion started with the conjunction of Saturn and Mercury approximately one and a half years earlier in May of 3 BC. When Mary told of the visit of Gabriel to her Uncle Zachariah during his once-in-a-lifetime duty in the Holy Place of the Jewish Temple, the magi nodded encouragingly. Simon, a party to the conversation could not help but blurt out, "Yes, a Jewish person of significance and a messenger from God, just as Master Gaspar thought."

Other parts of the puzzle then fell into place. Joseph stated that the conjunction of Saturn and Venus in June of 3 BC was on the morning of the day of his betrothal to Mary. Joseph's description of this event set off a warning bell in Gaspar's mind, but he could not place the reason for it.

The magi thought that the conjunction of Jupiter and Venus in August two months later indicated God's selection of Mary as the virgin to whom the Messiah would be born. After hearing this, Mary and Joseph were at first perplexed but then Mary remembered that the angel had described God's action as a choice made in the past, so perhaps this was correct. Later during that same month, the conjunction of Mercury and Venus was matched to the visit of the angel Gabriel to Mary, again as Gaspar had first thought, although now it was exceedingly joyful to place names of real persons with these conjunctions.

The three conjunctions of Jupiter and Regulus during the fall of 3 BC and winter and spring of 2 BC were unknown to Mary and Joseph. The magi explained that a triple conjunction of these two bodies was rare and a powerfully confirming sign, especially coming in the constellation of Leo, the symbol of the tribe of King David of Israel. Everyone knew what the next conjunction of Venus and Jupiter on June 17, 2 BC signified: the birth of Jesus! All those present thought back to that glorious and brilliantly lit night, and then looked at Jesus as he crawled and then attempted to stand.

Gaspar also asked when Joseph and Mary conducted her purification ceremony and learned that it had, indeed, occurred on July 28, the day of the conjunction of the sun and Regulus. Gaspar then stated that this ceremony, and the exclamation of Simeon and Anna, confirmed the prophesy of Daniel that proclaimed the arrival of the Messiah at the culmination of "62 sevens" of years.

As Gaspar was speaking, he suddenly realized what the conjunction of Saturn and Venus might mean on the day of Joseph and Mary's betrothal, and what had been bothering him all afternoon: Saturn, known as the Jewish Protectorate, likely signified Joseph. Joseph would likely be called on to protect the Jewish nation's savior. And then with a sickening realization, the intent of the magi's secret meeting with King Herod, a meeting without the chief priests and scribes, became clear to Gaspar. Herod intended to kill the child. As the magi bade Joseph and Mary farewell, Gaspar pulled Joseph aside and confided in him his grave concern.

> And being warned in a dream not to return to Herod, the [magi] departed to their own country by another way.

> Now when the [magi] had departed, behold, an angel of the Lord appeared to Joseph in a dream and said, "Rise, take the child and his mother, and flee to Egypt, and remain there till I tell you; for Herod is about to search for

> the child, to destroy him." And he rose and took the child and his mother by night, and departed to Egypt, and remained there until the death of Herod. This was to fulfill what the Lord had spoken by the prophet, "Out of Egypt have I called my son." [Matthew 2:12–15]

And Joseph worried as he traveled away from Bethlehem about the conjunction of Saturn and Venus that had heralded his betrothal to Mary. Gaspar's suspicions were confirmed by the angel's message. And Joseph hurried south into the night with his family.

> Then Herod, when he saw that he had been tricked by the wise men, was in a furious rage, and he sent [his guards] and [they] killed all the male children in Bethlehem and in all that region who were two years old or under, according to the time which he had ascertained from the wise men.[35] Then was fulfilled what was spoken by the prophet Jeremiah:
>
> > A voice was heard in Ramah, wailing and loud lamentation, Rachel weeping for her children; she refused to be consoled because they were no more.
>
> But when Herod died, behold, an angel of the Lord appeared in a dream to Joseph in Egypt, saying, "Rise, take the child and his mother, and go to the land of Israel, for those who sought the

> child's life are dead." And he rose and took the child and his mother, and went to the land of Israel. But when he heard that Archelaus reigned over Judea in place of his father, Herod, he was afraid to go there, and being warned in a dream he withdrew to the district of Galilee. And [Joseph and his family] went and dwelt in a city called Nazareth, that what was spoken by the prophets might be fulfilled, "[Jesus] shall be called a Nazarene." [Matthew 2:16–23]

The sixth Jewish month, Elul, 3 (August 20, 1 BC) in Babylon

Gaspar often wondered at what happened to Jesus, Mary and Joseph after he returned home and told his tale to the emperor. He and others became especially worried when stories circulated in the early spring of King Herod's orders to murder all young male children in the Bethlehem area shortly after they had left and then of King Herod's death. Could this be that the Messiah was cut off so very young, as only a baby?

In July of 1 BC, Venus arose in the evening from behind the Sun. Jupiter was on its usual route amongst the field of fixed stars, moving farther west each night. It was then when the first inkling of yet another possible conjunction between these two planets was broached among the magi and their apprentices. As August approached, the conjunction appeared to be more likely each night. On August 20, the conjunction occurred in the constellation Virgo.

"Is He safe, Master Gaspar?" said Simon, asking a question that had been heavy on the hearts of many since their journey.

"Simon, the heavens are telling the glory of God. And this conjunction between the king planet or Righteousness and the mother planet or Brightness allays my fears. The boy, Jesus, is safe in his mother's arms. Otherwise, we would not be seeing the firmament proclaiming God's handiwork.

"Will we ever see Jesus again, Master Gaspar?" asked Simon.

Gaspar responded, "Simon, I am an old man and unlikely to travel again, but perhaps when you return home to Cyrene after your apprenticeship, you may get the opportunity to see him again. I sense that in some small way you may even be able to help Jesus on his mission for our salvation."

Footnotes

31. Sometime during the summer/autumn of 2 BC, the star of Bethlehem seems to be lost as suggested in Matthew 2:10, in which he states that the magi were overjoyed at seeing the star. To a planetary scientist, however, planets "disappear" routinely. Planets rotate behind the sun from Earth's perspective for several weeks every year, that is, they are clothed in the sun, just as constellations are. Jupiter went behind the sun in late July of 2 BC because Earth rotates around the Sun more quickly than Jupiter does. This always occurs after Jupiter is visible in the evening skies, as was the case at

---

the birth of Jesus. Thus, Jupiter goes behind the sun, or disappears and rises again in the morning several weeks later, moves westward, again, until it "stops" against the field of fixed stars, as it does twice every year.

32. Did the Magi visit Jesus as described in Matthew 2:9–12 on or about December 25, 2 BC? Three lines of evidence support the idea that they did.

The first line of evidence is a synthesis of scripture and astronomy. Jupiter appeared to stop and stand over the place where the child was, as described in Matthew 2–9. Specifically, the planet Jupiter went into its annual backward motion in the year 2 BC by first stopping on or around December 25 and remaining stationary over the town of Bethlehem. This is definitive only when viewed from Jerusalem, which is where we know the magi were staying!

The second line of reasoning is actually quite simple, but only if one has an intimate knowledge of astronomy as many, if not all, of Matthew's readers did. Matthew states the obvious, that the star "stopped." This is a yearly occurrence for the planets visible to the naked eye because each has an orbit different from that of Earth's.

The third line of evidence is a synthesis of scripture and biology. The magi's visit is clearly some time after the birth of Jesus because the Greek words used by Matthew refer to a "house" and a "toddler." December 25 is about six months after Jesus' birth and, thus, the words *toddler* and *house* are consistent with Jesus' expected growth and Joseph securing more reasonable housing. Is it not also a nice touch that Jupiter stopped in the constellation Virgo, the Virgin?

33 Two of the gifts brought by the magi, gold and frankincense, were the gifts mentioned in Isaiah 60:6 that foreign kings would bring to Israel's Messiah

(http://www.versebyverse.org/doctrine/birthofchrist.html specifically, V. The Star of Bethlehem Identified, Who Were the Magi?).

34. I am indebted to Dwight Hutchinson (2013, page 207) for this insight.

35. The time of the first appearance of the star was August 12, 3 BC. Herod's decree for this murderous action was likely issued in January, 1 BC, approximately 18 months after the time of the star's first appearance that he obtained from his secret meeting with the magi.

EPILOGUE

This story theorizes that Jesus was born on what would have been June 17 of 2 BC. His birth occurred on the night of a full moon in the east and a Jupiter-Venus conjunction in the west. This conjunction was the brightest "star" anyone had likely ever seen before or likely since. His birth was 40 weeks to the day after his conception on September 11 3 BC, which was at the start of the Jewish holiday of Rosh Hashanah, the Day of Trumpets, when Virgo, the virgin, was clothed in the sun. His birth was preceded by seven conjunctions, two of which coincided with announcements by the angel, Gabriel, one to Zachariah, the Jewish priest to whom John the Baptist was born, and one to Mary, the virgin betrothed to Joseph. Jesus' birth was followed by another conjunction when the magi perhaps met with King Herod and the visit of the magi on a day when the planet Jupiter stood over the town of Bethlehem when viewed from Jerusalem, on what would have been December 25, 2 BC, or otherwise, the first Christmas.

Much has been written about the star of Bethlehem. I encourage the interested reader to check out several of these other texts, including:

- *The Lion Led the Way*, 2013, by Dwight Hutchinson. This is an incredibly well-researched book that emphasizes the Jewishness of Jesus' birth and the many signs in the heaven, many more than described in this story, that point to Jesus as the Messiah of the human race. *The Lion Led the Way* is an absolute must-read for any person wanting more information about this wonderful birth.
- *The First Christmas*, 2007, by Marcus Borg and John Dominic Crossasn and published by Harper One. This book emphasizes the parallels in the Gospels of Matthew and Luke to Old Testament writings. In addition, the authors draw surprising and insightful contrasts between the Roman way of establishing peace, typified by Caesar Augustus, and the way of peace of Jesus Christ.
- The Web site by Rick Larson, found at http://www.bethlehemstar.net, is a fountain of information regarding the star of Bethlehem and related events. Several of the events found in this story are based on this Web site. The site and accompanying video provide inspiration for those who seek even more confirmation of the theory presented in this story.

- *The Star That Astonished the World*, 1998, by Ernest Martin and published by Ask Publications. In many respects, this book was seminal to this story and perhaps other work, in that it promotes the idea that King Herod died in 1 BC, rather than 4 BC. A 1 BC death of King Herod allows us to consider many additional astronomical signs between 4 BC and 1 BC in our quest for understanding.

APPENDIX

The following four tables give additional information regarding the star of Bethlehem. Table 1, entitled "A Summary of the Star of Bethlehem Sequence," gives the chronological sequence of the events found in our story and converts the dates of all astronomical events into our Gregorian calendar. The specific dates of these astronomical events, with some slight changes, are given by Martin (1998). The chronology of events is found in the Bible.

Table 2, entitled "The 'Symbols' in the Star of Bethlehem Story," gives Jewish and Gentile names to the planets and constellations at the time of our story. These names are not exclusive, but several of them are commonly used today.

Table 3, entitled "Naked-Eye, Planet-Planet Conjunctions and Frequency of Favorable Visibility During the 21st Century," was used to estimate the number of years it would take for one of these conjunctions to occur and be visible from Earth. The resulting likelihood of these occurrences was stated throughout our story by Simon. The likelihood of these occurrences near the time of the star of Bethlehem may differ, although this difference is not expected to be great.

Frequencies are determined by dividing the number of conjunctions by 100 years, multiplying the result by the percentage of visibility, and then dividing by 2, for either an evening or morning conjunction. So, for example, Simon states in Chapter 1 that Saturn and Mercury have a morning conjunction once every 30 years. This is confirmed in Table 3 by dividing 124 conjunctions of Saturn and Mercury by 100 years, multiplying by the percentage of visibility, or 5 percent (or 0.05), and dividing by 2. The result is 0.03 conjunctions per year, or about one in every 30 years [124 ÷ 100 x 0.05 ÷ 2 = 0.03 conjunctions per year].

Table 4 is entitled "Approximate Gregorian Calendars for the Years 3 and 2 BC." Dates of the astronomical conjunctions in our story and Jewish holidays were mapped over to these calendars. Bold lettering indicates a conjunction; italic lettering indicates a Jewish holiday. These matches are not intended to be exact, especially because Jewish days start at sundown on the previous evening. Sharp eyes will see that these two years have the same Gregorian calendar dates as the years of 2009 and 2010.

Appendix Table 1. A Summary of the Star of Bethlehem Sequence.[a] All events have been converted to the Gregorian calendar (See Table 4).

Date / Time	Conjunction Constellation	Rough Chance	Event & Matching Biblical Text
20 May, 3 BC, morning	Mercury-Saturn in Taurus	1 in 30 years	The First Announcement of Gabriel (Mercury, God's Messenger) to Zachariah (Saturn, the Jewish Protectorate); Luke 1:8–20
13 June, 3 BC, morning	Venus-Saturn In Taurus	1 in 7 years	The Betrothal of Joseph (Saturn, the Jewish Protectorate) and Mary (Venus, Mother); Luke 1:27
12 August, 3 BC, morning	Jupiter-Venus in Cancer	1 in 12 years	First Observation of the Star Matthew 2:2; Numbers 24:17; Isaiah 60:3, II Peter 1:19, and Revelation 22:16
31 August, 3 BC, morning	Mercury-Venus in Leo	1 in 6 years	The Second Announcement of Gabriel (Mercury, God's Messenger), this time to Mary (Venus, Mother); Luke 1:26–37
11 September, 3 BC, evening	Sun clothes Virgo; crescent moon	1 per year	Conception of Jesus; constellation Virgo (Mary) is clothed by the sun (Father); Luke 1:35 and Revelation 12:1–2
14 September, 3 BC, morning	Jupiter-Regulus in Leo	1 in 38 years[b]	Jesus in the Womb; Jupiter (King planet) is in conjunction with Regulus (King star)
17 February, 2 BC, evening	Jupiter-Regulus in Leo		Jesus in the Womb; Jupiter (King planet) is in a second conjunction with Regulus (King star)
8 May, 2 BC, evening	Jupiter-Regulus in Leo		Jesus in the Womb; Jupiter (King planet) is in a third conjunction with Regulus (King star)

17 June, 2 BC, evening	Jupiter-Venus in Leo, full moon	1 in 12 years	Jesus is born; Jupiter (King) in conjunction with Venus (Mother); Luke 2:1–21
26 August, 2 BC, morning	Jupiter-Mars-Venus-Mercury in Leo	1 in 78 years	Visit of the magi in Jerusalem; conjunction of Mars (god of war), Jupiter (King), Venus (Mother), and Mercury (God's Messenger)
25 December, 2 BC, morning	Jupiter stops in Virgo	1 in 12 years	The star stops; the magi visit Jesus; Matthew 2:9–12

Footnotes

a. Based in part on Martin (1998, page 66) and in part on Stellarium © Stellarium 0.12.4, copyright 2000-2013 Stellarium Developers.

b. Based on Hutchinson (2013, page 187).

Table 2. The "Symbols" in the Star of Bethlehem Story

Object	Jewish Name; Meaning	Gentile Name (one of many)
Jupiter	Tzedek; righteousness or justice	King Planet
Leo	The constellation for the lion, associated with King David and the tribe of Judah	Lion
Mars	Ma'adim; blushing, reddening star	God of War
Mercury	Chammah; sun's scribe or attendant	God's Messenger
Moon	Yareach or Levanah	Luna
Regulus	Melech; king	King Star
Saturn	Shabbatei; rest or sabbatical	Jewish Protectorate
Sol (sun)	Shemesh or Chammah	Sol, Father
Venus	Nogah; brightness, brilliance radiance, splendor	Mother; Goddess of Fertility
Virgo	The constellation of Bethula; the virgin	Virgin

Table 3. Naked-Eye, Planet-Planet Conjunctions and Frequency of Favorable Visibility During the 21st Century

Percent Visibility →	Mercury	Venus	Mars	Jupiter	Saturn
Number of Conjunctions					
Mercury	-----------	13%	6%	13%	5%
Venus	237	----------	29%	17%	29%
Mars	153	79	----------	33%	28%
Jupiter	125	98	45	----------	20%
Saturn	124	104	50	5	----------

Generally, Mercury's number of conjunctions with other planets decreases as one examines the planets outward to Saturn. The reverse occurs for the other planets (event frequency increases outward). Percent favorable visibility simply means the percentage of events that can be seen from Earth. Thus, only 13 percent of the 237 Mercury-Venus conjunctions in the 21st century can be seen, resulting, for example, in a "once in six years" frequency in the evenings.

Table 4 (on the following pages). Approximate Gregorian Calendars for the Years 3 and 2 BC. (*Italic, gray dates* = Jewish holiday; Bold dates = conjunctions per Table 1.)

January 3 BC						
Su	Mo	Tu	We	Th	Fr	Sa
				1	2	3
4	5	6	7	8	9	10
11	12	13	14	15	16	17
18	19	20	21	22	23	24
25	26	27	28	29	30	31

February 3 BC						
Su	Mo	Tu	We	Th	Fr	Sa
1	2	3	4	5	6	7
8	9	10	11	12	13	14
15	16	17	18	19	20	21
22	23	24	25	26	27	28

May 3 BC						
Su	Mo	Tu	We	Th	Fr	Sa
					1	2
3	4	5	6	7	8	9
10	11	*Festival of weeks>*				*16*
17	*18*	*19*	**20**	*21*	*22*	23
24	25	26	27	28	29	30
31						

June 3 BC						
Su	Mo	Tu	We	Th	Fr	Sa
	1	2	3	4	5	6
7	8	9	10	11	12	**13**
14	15	16	17	18	19	20
21	22	23	24	25	26	27
28	29	30				

September 3 BC						
Su	Mo	Tu	We	Th	Fr	Sa
		1	2	3	4	5
6	*Rosh Hashanah>*				**11**	*12*
13	**14**	15	16	17	18	19
20	*21*	*<Yom Kippur*			*25*	*26*
27	*28*	*29*	*30*	*<Tabernacles*		

October 3 BC						
Su	Mo	Tu	We	Th	Fr	Sa
				1	2	3
4	5	6	7	8	9	10
11	12	13	14	15	16	17
18	19	20	21	22	23	24
25	26	27	28	29	30	31

March 3 BC						
Su	Mo	Tu	We	Th	Fr	Sa
1	2	3	4	5	6	7
8	9	10	11	12	13	14
15	16	17	18	19	20	21
22	23	24	Passover>			28
29	30	31				

April 3 BC						
Su	Mo	Tu	We	Th	Fr	Sa
			1	2	3	4
5	6	7	8	9	10	11
12	13	14	15	16	17	18
19	20	21	22	23	24	25
26	27	28	29	30		

July 3 BC						
Su	Mo	Tu	We	Th	Fr	Sa
			1	2	3	4
5	6	7	8	9	10	11
12	13	14	15	16	17	18
19	20	21	22	23	24	25
26	27	28	29	30	31	

August 3 BC						
Su	Mo	Tu	We	Th	Fr	Sa
						1
2	3	4	5	6	7	8
9	10	11	**12**	13	14	15
16	17	18	19	20	21	22
23	24	25	26	27	28	29
30	**31**					

November 3 BC						
Su	Mo	Tu	We	Th	Fr	Sa
1	2	3	4	5	6	7
8	9	10	11	12	13	14
15	16	17	18	19	20	21
22	23	24	25	26	27	28
29	30					

December 3 BC						
Su	Mo	Tu	We	Th	Fr	Sa
		1	2	3	4	5
6	7	8	9	10	11	12
13	14	15	16	17	18	19
20	21	22	23	24	25	26
27	28	29	30	31		

January 2 BC						
Su	Mo	Tu	We	Th	Fr	Sa
					1	2
3	4	5	6	7	8	9
10	11	12	13	14	15	16
17	18	19	20	21	22	23
24	25	26	27	28	29	30
31						

February 2 BC						
Su	Mo	Tu	We	Th	Fr	Sa
	1	2	3	4	5	6
7	8	9	10	11	12	13
14	15	16	**17**	18	19	20
21	22	23	24	25	26	27
28						

May 2 BC						
Su	Mo	Tu	We	Th	Fr	Sa
						1
2	3	4	5	6	7	**8**
9	10	11	12	13	14	15
16	17	18	19	20	21	22
23	24	25	26	27	28	29
30	31					

June 2 BC						
Su	Mo	Tu	We	Th	Fr	Sa
		Festival of weeks>				5
6	*7*	*8*	*9*	*10*	*11*	12
13	14	15	16	**17**	18	19
20	21	22	23	24	25	26
27	28	29	30			

September 2 BC						
Su	Mo	Tu	We	Th	Fr	Sa
			1	2	3	4
5	6	7	8	9	10	11
12	13	14	15	16	17	18
19	20	21	22	23	24	25
Rosh Hashanah>				*30*		

October 2 BC						
Su	Mo	Tu	We	Th	Fr	Sa
					1	2
3	4	5	*Yom Kippur>*			*9*
10	*Tabernacles>*			*14*	*15*	*16*
17	*18*	*19*	*20*	21	22	23
24	25	26	27	28	29	30
31						

March 2 BC						
Su	Mo	Tu	We	Th	Fr	Sa
	1	2	3	4	5	6
7	8	9	10	11	12	13
14	15	16	17	18	19	20
21	22	23	24	25	26	27
28	29	30	31			

April 2 BC						
Su	Mo	Tu	We	Th	Fr	Sa
				1	2	3
4	5	6	7	8	9	10
11	12	13	*Passover>*			*17*
18	*19*	*20*	*21*	*22*	*23*	24
25	26	27	28	29	30	

July 2 BC						
Su	Mo	Tu	We	Th	Fr	Sa
				1	2	3
4	5	6	7	8	9	10
11	12	13	14	15	16	17
18	19	20	21	22	23	24
25	26	27	28	29	30	31

August 2 BC						
Su	Mo	Tu	We	Th	Fr	Sa
1	2	3	4	5	6	7
8	9	10	11	12	13	14
15	16	17	18	19	20	21
22	23	24	25	**26**	27	28
29	30	31				

November 2 BC						
Su	Mo	Tu	We	Th	Fr	Sa
	1	2	3	4	5	6
7	8	9	10	11	12	13
14	15	16	17	18	19	20
21	22	23	24	25	26	27
28	29	30				

December 2 BC						
Su	Mo	Tu	We	Th	Fr	Sa
			1	2	3	4
5	6	7	8	9	10	11
12	13	14	15	16	17	18
19	20	21	22	23	24	**25**
26	27	28	29	30	31	

ABOUT THE AUTHOR

Michael Leonard Dourson has a doctoral degree in toxicology from the University of Cincinnati, College of Medicine. He is the president of Toxicology Excellence for Risk Assessment, a non-profit consultancy on environmental health issues. He also leads Bible study classes at Mt. Zion Lutheran Church in Lucas, Ohio, and through this activity, discovered a love of integrating science concepts with Biblical text. *Messiah's Star* is the first book in a series devoted to this love.

Michael is happily married to his first wife, Martha, a farmer's daughter, turned lawyer. They have 3 lovely children, two lovely children-in-law, and one grandson. Mike now considers himself fortunate to be number 7 on Martha's list.

Besides gardening, fishing, and publishing (mostly science papers), Michael is active in developing the next generation of scientists and Christians devoted to a fulfilling life.

Michael welcomes your thoughts. You may contact him at http://messiahsstar.com

NOTES

NOTES

NOTES

NOTES

NOTES

Made in the USA
Charleston, SC
17 June 2014